Peter Sansom was born in 1958 in Nottinghamshire. Carcanet published his first book in 1990, a Poetry Book Society Recommendation. Other titles include *Selected Poems* and *Careful What You Wish For*, which won him the Cholmondeley Award in 2016. He has been Fellow in Poetry at Leeds and Manchester Universities, and Company Poet for M&S and The Prudential. With Ann Sansom, Peter is a director of the Poetry Business in Sheffield and co-editor of *The North* magazine and Smith/Doorstop Books.

LANYARD

PETER SANSOM

CARCANET POETRY

LANYARD

'A short length of rope for securing something'
– OED

*'And I could panic that all my relatives are gone,
only alive in flashes of anecdote'*
– Stanley Cook

First published in Great Britain in 2022 by
Carcanet
Alliance House, 30 Cross Street
Manchester, M2 7AQ
www.carcanet.co.uk

A CIP catalogue record for this book is
available from the British Library.

ISBN   978 1 80017 020 9

Book design by Andrew Latimer
Printed in Great Britain by SRP Ltd, Exeter, Devon

The publisher acknowledges financial
assistance from Arts Council England.

CONTENTS

ACKNOWLEDGEMENTS

Thanks are due to the editors of the following magazines where several of the poems first appeared, *The Manchester Review*, *PN Review*, *The Rialto*, *Stand*, *Under the Radar*, *What Do You Mean*, *Who Do You Think You Are*, and Jonathan Davidson's Out of Office email response. The poem 'Brian' is a slightly revised version of 'Clinical Depression', which appeared in my collection *Point of Sale* (Carcanet 2000) and which seems to fit into the story of the present book. For the same reason I've taken the liberty of reprising 'Mini Van' from *Careful What You Wish For* (Carcanet 2015) – and which gives me chance, too, to thank Neil Astley for including it in *Staying Human* (Bloodaxe, 2020).

LANYARD

KING'S MILL

I

This is the then I stand in now: a map
of Mansfield to Sutton far as Derbyshire
pinned up on a wall. Here's the A38,
a three-mile missed-bus walk back from The Crown
with its weed and coolest juke box ('See Emily Play',
'Twenty-first Century Schizoid Man'). The lake on it is
King's Mill reservoir (of not-for-drinking water)
which my friend sailed, and I swam in once, Moon River
after the exams and before the results, six of us
ignoring the signs – the splash and gasp of it still.
Twenty years later I walked its grey midweek round
with my brother (this very clearly like a dream)
and back to his locked ward, a year into the breakdown
after Vera died. In our family we stay married.

That other King's Mill, the hospital, is marked here too.
I remember its corridors, vending machines,
the other machines, and Mum, still herself,
though sometimes her dad had just left;
and later my sister, those foam sticks of water
I brought to her lips that couldn't keep her alive.
They all lived here in time, another brother
though only briefly, quite suddenly dying
of pneumonia, the old man's friend – when I arrived,
breathless, the cousin I asked which ward
told me with a smile the morgue, and I never thought
to hit him till now, and still don't really,
dead these days as he is too. Map on a wall
I take down, like moving home, clearing out.

II

In its folds, Skegby to Hardwick, and on the back
through Sherwood to Newstead. There's Byron's gaff
with my dad in a home a mile from it next door.
In one of those lucid moments ('Should you go, Tony?')
he let himself be taken. I visited just once,
with all the time in the world, though I ran past it
through the forest all the time with Sutton Harriers.
More than dad I remember the paths that follow
under leaf sky, the days when I was good enough
to make up the numbers on their cinder track,
in that proud non-descript vest. A coincidence
it was their social club for my sister's Ruby wedding.

How flat a map is, coming down, coming to this end,
despite the contours, which flourish, which break out,
pastoral or at any rate not built up. White desert
of a colliery. And with it, what that's come to mean,
which once was the rumble of our Johnno delivering
coal on the QT at eleven at night, the fire banked-up
for Steve Davies on the telly, or the classmate
met shocking in the precinct: me one year into college
and him ten years older from the pit at Teversal.

III

I look and it's all here. The M1 runs out South
to the big noise, the road to somebody's success,
and North in time for us to the M18
and happy Cleethorpes, the kids just as they were.
Map on a wall. My childhood. Theirs.
Map of the back of my hand, of my head,
the me my me my of an ambulance,
or a body of water to stand beside, to look out on
shifting without moving to stand here
pinning a map up and one lifetime later
taking it down. And seeing through it into
a locked sliding door, or breeze-touched waves
that never reach our feet, and which even so
we walk into, gasping, just as we are.

and once round the gasometer. Tony's jumper.
Also larger than life his donkey jacket
and boots in the cupboard under the stairs
with a pair of wellingtons like waders.
Road drill for the gas-board, he played dominoes
in the Traveller's of a Sunday at Hucknall
and everybody knew him, though the ones
who kept him alive by remembering
are dead themselves or other people now.
That generation who never learned to drive
stayed put or only moved in walking distance.
A bottle at Christmas with tenners in the wrapping,
that was him, when tenners were fifties. Delighted,
Mum said 'I might have put that on the friggin fire'
though in the flat it was central heating.
She was born 1914. Dad in nineteen ought four.
They thought the electric would leak out like gas.
Tony didn't explain, only stepped in. Likewise
digging a neighbour's garden against doctor's orders
proved he couldn't live forever. Even so, here he is
with the whole clan taking that jumper off
upstairs in the Denman's for Chubby Checker,
like we did last summer, a wedding anniversary
or somebody's 21st. He was 21
when I was born. I was Tony's brother,
that's who I was. If I put his jumper on now,
and his coat, and those boots like boats
they'd swamp me. And his wellingtons, I'd never get out.

Hello and *Take a Break* are all 'My Holiday
Cancer' and 'I Married a Serial Killer', so
without even checking the horoscopes
coughing and trying not to cough
I turn to *Ideal Home* and recognise the centrefold
of IKEA shelving and that stalk-headed Mac
in the stylish home office. Leafing through
is fast-forward, just-hoovered, a smell of paint.
Always a book propped open, surprising,
and always a smiling woman, less so,
so I check coughing and trying not to
and yes, not one man only that stick figure
in the lawnmower ad. The first pages coughing
are all ads, cookers and freezers dearer
than our car till here, 'Fresh Looks That Last'.
Likewise in this September when I was fifty
and thought I was old, 'How to Preserve the Sun
in Summer Fruit.' The number trying not
to cough in the air and on the screen's
not mine. Nobody meets my eye in this
coughing stopped-clock mid-week rush,
and I wonder how many have actually died
in an underfunded waiting room,
before lighting on *Cosmo*, with its once
jaw-dropping agony column back
when sex was everything, and everything
effing coughing was ha ha still possible.

ROOFER & SON

Two degrees from freezing and here they are
in their website t-shirts to see where the rain
is getting in this time. His lad who will be his lad
at forty holds the ladder foot with his boot

while he swings a cat-ladder onto the slates.
Some people thrive up there. They sit higher,
much higher, with sandwiches and look
at a different town to us. A friend of a friend

earns a week in a day dangling from bridges
and thousand-foot ledges, safe as houses
if you trust your kit and out of body self.
I see that. Like the crane driver, which was

my ambition, who sees everything unseen
from his lunar module. But at twenty
I ran up a ladder to the roof as usual
after a storm meaning to turn the aerial

when some chemical flicked a switch
and I was stuck at the guttering grip-
ping the top rung. Gripping the top rung.
I'd be there still if you hadn't come along.

COMPREHENSIVE

I

You stand at the blackboard,
which is all there was then, chalk
on your jacket and in your unruly hair.
In a metal-frame window an all-weather pitch
and playing fields far as the pit head
and a Norman church scaled small to touch.
Also, the full moon in broad day
that any one of us, the great deprived,
might walk on in the age of social welfare.

II

Through ash woods that gave the town its name
a path wound at New Year to snowy
Hardwick Hall, or its grounds. Someone
with a cassette of Nicely Out of Tune, *when
winter's shadowy fingers* and though
the woods were empty, there you were
amo, amas, and at your heels the geese
that saved an empire, and tie-dye, and books,
the endless opportunity of words.

III

It was a step (the 1944 Education Act) and it
brought us somewhere, for a while, assembled,
a psalm and he who would valiant be.

IV

Decades later, the moon further than ever,
I wake in sweat from our day together
at the coast. It was the hottest summer.
I was old enough to know. It made you human,
even now I wake and you're ten years dead,
we park on the promenade, two people
in the late afternoon. Sun and moon
in the same sky. We walk on the beach, the day
behind us and the clear-eyed night ahead.
Sand in our shoes and our shoes in our hands,
we walk fully clothed into the sea.

BRIAN

I drove thirty virtuous miles
with the dozen years of our growing up,
to say I'm here and sit with him in the dayroom
once a week for a month, though he was there
longer. Brother. Half-brother.
Film star cheekbones from Dad's side
and the thin mouth, wet eyes. One day
we walked by the res across the road.
Sailing boats, their nodding masts. Boys went by
on mountain bikes, and we talked and got nowhere,
in the end back to the block he suddenly
can't believe is right. He knows I get things wrong,
so has to see my car in the carpark,
see the key fit the lock before he'll try
the automatic doors, the corridors and still
there's a panic not to be wrong, at last to read
the curious ward name and know he's home.
Which is when I'm stopped by the ECT
he signed himself to. What do I know?
His sister thought it would work, they had to
try something. And as she pointed out later,
'cheaper than drugs, cheaper than talk'
that's just politics, and this is not about me,
and his wife, whatever you say, every night,
every morning, will stay dead.

WHITBY

St Hilda's Priory, Sneaton

Six no seven tractors, and two shire horses
that trudge over, mistaking me.

A polytunnel, a nuns' cats' cemetery,
and far on the hill above the Esk
the Abbey, with the famous steps
up to St Mary's, counting all the way.

Caedmon's there if you think that way
mucking out in a snowbound winter
and dreaming the first poem.

*

St Mary's Churchyard

Another time just then and there
a nice American asked which
was Dracula's grave.
I said I didn't know but told my friends
I showed him a stone-washed sepulchre,
quite blank among the leaning stones.
And when all's said no less real
than the Venerable Bede
or for that matter these bare trees,
ruined choirs of a seminar
where late the sweet birds sang,
in one ear and out the other.

*

Sonnet 73

I can sit on a bench by this
stained glass window
as the boy I was one afternoon
when the lights came on

in a tutor's room in the Poly.
I loved that place.
That was me, whose brother
never learned to read.

We bowed our heads
in the long black window
to our books. And today *that time*
of year thou may'st in me behold

on this bench, with my brother
in my head whom I never
taught to read dead a dozen years,
and the poem I still know

still there too. I say it under
my breath, who knows why.

Barbara and Derek, Derek and Barbara and Dinah,
the collie dog, who rode the B-roads and by-roads
of retirement from a house of windows and a carport
in the Rolls Royce of campervans, with a love of words
and passing places, the wide-open spaces
of a gazetteer. I was eighteen,
a friend of their missing son. Miles unrolled
in birdsong through the low gears of going on,
each hill steeper up or down. Night was all talk,
Blue-jean Derek, Jean-Paul Derek, nervy
Gitanes fingers, Blue Oyster Cult sweatshirt
and John Berryman beard. And Barbara
like an aunt, brilliant in a travel-ironed blouse
with plenty that she didn't need to say.
We parked by lochs for the morning view,
strolled by the salmon ladder in Pitlochry,
and shared the last of summer on a site for once
with others, fishing rods and deck-chair beach-books.
At Inverness Ian Anderson my Jo ran up
the backs of raked seats with a flute, and one afternoon
a helicopter, Nicky B Mason of the Pink Floyd.
But that was the brightness, the noise in a month
of roving stillness, of living then-ness, bee-glade calm.
Each night, Derek wrote the ship's log of each day,
pine forest, a tiny lake called a tarn, some very funny joke,
a hand of Canasta, all new. The middle class. So that
in locum filium one sunlit night walk, I looked out
from the Kyle of Lochalsh, across a not-yet-built bridge
to the cut-out Skye in its ending, and I could walk there

even at that distance, because of what they taught me.
I never thanked you, but I thank you now,
a decade too late, Barbara and Derek,
Derek and Barbara and Dinah the dog.

ON FIRST HEARING 'CARELESS WHISPER'

I knew I knew it, just couldn't bring it to mind.
It was like love at first sight and, with Keats
for a pillow, almost a remembrance. Devon,
another hot day, the day before the rain, a radio
on a caravan site above a bay. August,
that holiday I first read Frank O'Hara ('The waves
stopped me from reaching you', 'The Day Lady Died')
and saw *And Then There Were None* in a village hall.
What a voice you had. They played it in the interval,
and a man I didn't know asked me. Then it was
everywhere, betrayal made-over by regret.
Hearing it today, driving, the wipers going,
even just the opening bars, I'm stopped
on a cliff-edge, you, me and everybody
in our twenties. Next day it rained, so much
we called it a day, that buddy and me, packed
the sodden tent up, packed ourselves up, set off
the endless drive back with nothing to say.
I held the wheel from the passenger seat
in the slow lane while he dozed, too young
to see the danger and anyway what was it,
the wipers going, the radio on,
the opening bars, that saxophone.

BEYOND HARLECH

Referendum Result Day

In the sun everything was fine, drifting
from castle to café with the local paper
and a thriller from the library sale.
A short dazzling walk down the coast
till here was heart-lift, a bay
that began with an L, two ells of course,
golden beyond Harlech, where a couple
strolled like an ad from a campervan
called California. The mountains
make the bay a suntrap. The woman
who said this wanted me to sign
a petition: a mind-set from the sixties
when people could change and change
the world, and yes she had a flower
in her grey hair (a slide). English,
she came to paint while there was time.
And so it was that I stood
with sparkling water in a beach cafe
far from the/at the centre of the
world with her friends and fellow petitioners,
while the world went to hell, or our
little bit of it, and of course America.
And yet how happy we were.
It was like being in an Alice Munro story.
Someone did a course with my friend Gerard
just up the road, and even that day,
and even though Gerard's dead,
I couldn't not be happy. For twenty minutes
a nice man talked to me in Welsh

and I found myself nodding in complete,
baffled agreement, glad to have
added my name to their campaign,
while the last request stop train went by.

BIKE RIDE

I scoot the pedal, self-conscious, and swing on,
set off, past choir at the Methodist Mission
and the C of E foodbank and the shell
of Stanley's Works and across Stanley's Field
like a bowling green where nobody comes out
at dinner time kicking a ball. By Wood Fold
then through the wood, ticking past celandine
and condom wrappers, not taking the path up
to the burned down Ski Village (despite the view
of the Peak, first to get and last to lose the snow);
then like a boy to let go the brakes and
hold on tight, freewheel the steep track past
body shops, UPVC and a born-again woodturners,
the prefab wind-down years of light industry
and computer aided design, and to burst out
from under the disused railway, and past
the derelict brewery, that tree of wild apples,
that garage, and to feel at home on a bike
for the first time in thirty years: till levelling
off, slowing, nearly stopping – strait being the gate
onto a tow-path – I find myself under a cliff-face
of mill apartments, where a window cleaner
abseils to the sky in a weir. Just beyond,
a rowing boat's moored like a thought
to borrow and step unsteady into; but no,
I coast on, a young man for all I know
until at Pitsmoor Road the hill will have me
get off and walk. Till then a cycle path
peek into these lives beside the river, as if
they were there to join, have a second go,
the most of it on the level by a gallery
of balconies, some with teapots, some with bikes.

IT'D BEEN ROUND THE CLOCK, TWICE MAYBE, AND THE GUY

did the test drive himself, then put it on a ramp,
gift-horse or death-trap, who knew. Three doors, four gears
and several careless owners, we paid to have it rebuilt
as it fell to bits, clutch, brake-pedal, the wishbone,

whatever that was, and WD40 every wet morning
for the spark plugs, and when the seal went the velour
smelt like something had died. A pimple in the windscreen
opened like a waterfall to replace at our own expense, and, yes,

even the engine, by the garage that sold it us. And yet
we loved it. First love, us and the kids, the three of them
squashed to the roof on sleeping bags too big
for the tiny boot the night we just set off, arriving

in the small hours to pitch two tents somewhere
by Wastwater, remotest and deepest, under
a moonless brilliant sky right next we saw
in the morning to Strictly No Camping. Those years

we drove miles, bad judgement, good karma,
the length and breadth of holiday and work, work, work,
and never a penny richer. There's no doubt
it was a metaphor.

HALIFAX

In the midst of life we are in Halifax

I know this view. I've lived it, on my own,
then with a mate, then with my wife, then
with my wife and kids. I know it on Platform 3
where you breathe in Rowntrees and look round.
Then there's EUREKA and man-handling a foot
ball game from the Piece Hall onto the bus.
We laugh out loud, embarrassing, their mum and me,
at a Colemanballs book from a charity shop.
Hurt is still an idea far enough away. Everywhere
is steep, even the precinct, Smiths and Boots
before the blackened cliff you have to go
a long way round. Mills are shopping or art,
the canal's a narrowboat and lunch hour sandwich,
while the indoor market has stalls that go back
two hundred years, and forward far as 1990.
I try it again for fruit and vinyl, a pair of socks
and a quarter of sherbet lemons. Poverty doesn't
bear thinking about, so I stand in the must
of secondhand books, and choose coloured glass
for a present. A friend owns sheep on that close-cropped hill
and a train leaves like sleepwalking. I bet he's on it.
This is me waving, and not just me either.

ECG

In a check-up for teacher training
the doctor heard a murmur,
'Come back next year and we'll see.'
Forty years later she's suddenly
young enough to be my daughter

and abandons what turns out to be
pneumonia in favour of an ECG.
Of course I know hearts stop, so many have
just in my lifetime, friends, relatives,
all those celebrities. Mine apparently

has got it into its head to race.
I say 'Well, you've not met my wife.'
Which is why I'm lying here staring
at a striplight, holding my breath.
A day or two later they unpeel the wires

and help me down, but keep me seated
in case the slightest effort kills me.
Then I wait for the specialist in hearts,
a poet no doubt, to tell me
what I don't need to know.

WEATHERMAN

A breath becomes a brisk north-easterly
turning the wheel that turns the han-
dle and the wooden man
bobs to his task. Easily

moved, going nowhere, unaware,
sleeves rolled whatever
the weather, when he can
he stops and stands like anyone

would to look across the fields, to gauge
just where he is. Weather vane,
whirligig, fixed to the prow
of the shed he figureheads. A brown

blackbird lands beside him on the roof
then drops to listen to the lawn.
A gust and she's off, and he's off,
a cog in the machine

of this October morning.
His black hair is dyed, his red cardie
ridiculously cheery. Who is he,
stitching the hours with nothing

to show for it, turning the wind-
mill of the wind.

ROOM

Some way after one of the personas of Fernando Pessoa

The end of the day, I climb up to this room.
They bring a lamp and say goodnight, and I hear
my voice say goodnight, and I forget them.
And for the idea of it make a drink, then settle here
by the window and look out on the street,
houses, a streetlight, and people coming back
from wherever they've been. As if time and people
might let you do it again, do it right, make amends.
I sit with a book but I'm not reading. The day
flows by me, dry river to the sea. Friends
and colleagues, a whole family seems to know me.
Another time a prayer might be said, but nothing's said,
not even, what is it, this. I came here on a whim.
I climbed a ladder to a room and found him.

GERARD BENSON
for Cathy

You were a good age as Dad would say;
like him, mid-eighties, but still young and still
knowing your own quick and open-hearted mind
while your body closed down round you. Those last days
I visited with the proofs of your memoir –
from sent away to Wales to brought nameless back
to gas masks, boy chaperone to a wayward aunt
dancing with her beau (afterwards cake
in a Lyons). ASM, you understudied in rep,
your triumph a walk-on lamplighter
who stole a laugh from nothing, which turned out
the story of your life. You caught the sixties full-on
with the thinking man's crumpet and your own show
at the RFH. Your Barrow Poets' single
topped the Australian charts. Who knew
when you arrived in town with your poet's moll,
your Poems on the Underground and your books
for Penguins, in your natty old-fashioned hat. You strolled
a furled umbrella into our Northern rain
and became its laureate. I loved your work
and like everybody didn't see just how good it is.

POETRY SOCIETY

i.m. Sarah Maguire

Sarah half a lifetime ago I met you
in a meeting at the top of Betterton Street.
I remember your tank-commander's watch
exactly an hour wrong. You were one year older
and half a lifetime further on. I think
we made each other frivolous, though you
were serious in your art, just as I imagine
in how you lived. So many spoke
because of you. Except for poems I only knew
you were a gardener. Your project
was nurturing also, a public space, your words
there in the soil, so many cuttings and changings.
A sort of translation. You said translation
was the opposite of war. We said our paths
must cross in this small world, but I met you again
only in poems, your own, unmistakable, and
those Latin names gathered in *Flora Poetica*,
the real meaning of anthology. Opening it today
is to step into bright shade, so many perfumes
and the promise where no day was, though
in that society there was a roof to sit out on
in the sun to talk and drink and read
in the middle of London, in the middle
of all those words and reputations – your own
not least now your work outlives you
all that unbelievable short time ago.

PNEUMONIA

I coughed for a month with no idea,
till the doctor put me on something stronger
(he didn't know I was taking
my germs to work). He was a boy
with the same manner as our eldest,
which gave me pause. Which gives me pause.
The next was older, dapper, met my eye:
'We'll try a different course and then
it's either the hospital or the crem.'
And so I went to bed and didn't die
of pneumonia, the old man's friend
that killed my brother at seventy.
Also Louis MacNeice, a friend pointed out
pleased, years younger than me,
was I still thinking of being somebody.
It's not a competition, as T S Eliot said
(by then he'd won the Nobel Prize), though
it's true I've lived longer than I thought
and not done as well as I hoped.

PHONE CALL

No one uses the landline
except scams and those relatives
in living memory of *putting you
through now caller*, and sure enough
it's my sister. Except she died
years ago, ten years ago, tired
of going to bed early with the telly.

Still, it's her, for a moment, so
Maureen I say *it's great to hear you.*
I don't remember ever saying that
though she was my favourite, they
all were, but Maureen brought me up,
and then there's Auntie Tad
and Auntie Olive too who loved me
so much I still have the birthday mug
You're The Cream In My Coffee
with a stave to sing in your head
when you made a drink. There's a photo
somewhere of Maureen's dog
with its head in that mug. I remember
she paid the earth each month
for its haircut. It made us smile
though we had no money either,

which makes me think that where
we spend it says who we are, that
and all the time that goes with it.
I want to say something to Maureen,
something more than words, but of course
it's her daughter I don't say it to.

ALFRETON AND MANSFIELD PARKWAY, JUNE EVENING

Miles from Mansfield
and not close to Alfreton,
with one prefab waiting room
and a vending machine Out of Order.

Three drunk women are fighting
on the Nottingham platform,
in the same pair of glasses, owls
out on the town. They could be

my sisters. A train comes in
and they stop like actors
between scenes. On they get,
off they go. Trees line-side

step back into pony pasture
and thistles, the lovers' lane
of Strawberry Bank
where my mother walked

in a photo when this halt
was for the pit in Lawrence,
before my sisters were thought of,
before they ever lived and died.

'TO THE WATERFALLS'

Having taken advantage
of the disc parking, I stride out
under green-tunnel trees
down the cool summer lane
to the waterfalls. Who could resist
a sign like that, an arrow
straight out of Robin Hood
and handwriting like dad's,
all that generation, who left school
at twelve and wrote in ink,
their names upright, stately.
Walkers course by with their hellos
and now here's a second path.
When it ends at a bench
I sit for the view and know
I never knew him.
Born nineteen ought four
as he liked to say it he was retired
before he told me one story,
about Bluey and Greeny,
the marbles. A surprise
afterwards to hear eg he played
mouth organ round the pubs.
I think about the Labour Club
and the Staff of Life.
How little I've thought about his life
and how circumscribed I see it is
now he lives it again as me.

MINI VAN

In the back, with no seats or windows,
just more grey metal. In the end I curl up
on my coat and listen to the road smooth
and bumpy, slow till he puts his foot down
on the new by-pass by Hucknall. This was where
mum worked before the war, a butcher's sooner
than be in service. Though I don't know it yet.
And we're still alive, both of us.
Unseen dark-eyed trees are a way home

through Sherwood Forest, where one day
I'll run with the harriers. But I'm not
a teenager yet, and this is Mick's van,
our Mick driving us large as life
from Nottingham to a houseful of the dead
still living in Sutton, Sutton-in-Ashfield,
one winter Saturday, with the tea just mashed
and a bit of dinner waiting for us.

I'm tired of everyone being dead.
I'm tired of being in this van.

RACEDOWN

He leaps the gate, his party piece, and cuts
the corner of a pathless field. She looks up,
waves a trowel, and calls to her brother. Smiles.
She's twenty-five and will remember this
the rest of her days, even when most of the days
are lost: Coleridge as he was. Closer to,
soup-stained, and with a days-long odour.
He walked city to city talking all the way.
But what she sees is how he listened to her.
They are orphans together minding a child
in a borrowed house; they read to each other
through the night and talk about the sea.
Next day they set off in their newly-wedded lives,
the three of them, to the mountains and the lakes,
where we look out for them with their books.

ULLSWATER

The steamer took silver from the foot of Helvellyn
and now takes us to Aira Force and Gowbarrow
where Dorothy taught William to see daffodils.
The lake goes far as the mind can see. The mountains
keep their snow and take no notice. We walked there,
St Sunday Crag and, somewhere, Brothers Water
with its story; but that was yesterday, the ice-age,
and it's this black, in-the-moment depth of water
that we motor out on in our beanie hats and scarves.
It's talent or it's luck; it's character or it's fate. Stand, step
from a wind-chilled ferry in February unsteady
into a rowing boat one schoolboy summer night
in this vale of Patterdale, so still the oars echo, ripple
down the years, heavy but you get the hang of it,
and pull through the stolen darkness. Put your back
into it, your skill, then pause. Listen to the night, your back
to the water. Listen, your face to the rising fell.
The sky's black or the sky's awash with stars;
the moon's full or there's no moon. Set your mind
to it and your heart, feel the smooth roughness
where your palms will blister, and row, come on,
keep going, back to those you love, it's endless.

THE STRUGGLE

A road that unwinds
from Kirkstone in low
gear, one-in-five, the bends
hair-raising in drizzle
and impassable in snow.

A farmer broadcasts bright
blue pellets and sheep
come bounding. I pull into
a nook not a passing place
of a sudden to walk on the moon

off-message for a while
in the blustery sun, the good news
still in my still-hippy head.
A mile away, the stationary blast
of a waterfall, and there

a day on Windermere
when we were starting out
and could joke about the pun
in rowing. Too late
for that far red dot

to be delivering post to
our little place in The Lakes –
too late, but I'm rich I tell
the mountains in other ways.
Oh yes indeed they say

though it sounds like baa.

PIGEONS

'Sometimes to someone pigeon fanciers,
Backyard mechanics, rabbit breeders,
Hermit chrysanthemum growers on allotments
And trumpet players in silver prize bands
Are/were/will be great'
– Stanley Cook

Who'd have thought that doves were pigeons or,
nicer, the other way round. Vermin of the air,
pickers-up in olden times of fag butts in precincts,
scatterers of seeds and followers of ploughs – pigeons,
whose droppings, look, wreck paintwork. That one,
just-landed up there, might have borne the olive branch.
I hope so – with Ararat our roof and the chimney
he looks out from solid ground at last, plain sailing.

Favourite is the pigeon we saw in Pepe's cafe
with the youngest that day when her beautiful
infallible mother announced, 'Look at that penguin.'
A family saying now, 'Look at that penguin.'

Who'd have thought that suddenly it's this year
and here we are with the youngest, the teacher,
by the pigeon cotes at Sky Edge. We stand in the sun
and look, her whole childhood later, at a swirl
of birds in the blue above Park Hill. Then a man
who might be my brother, the one who never
went to school, arrives to let us know all about them.

His dark eyes glitter, seeing them again
in the telling, not the baskets and pantechnicon,
but the start of the flying, when it's not racing
but homing, from as far away as France,
and what he wants to tell us is that moment
that spectacular moment when they're set free
in their hundreds to fill and more than fill the sky.

And equally, here on this one of Sheffield's seven hills,
what he wants to tell us is him, himself, here waiting,
at the far end of the journey. When there she is,
his favourite, unmistakable in all that sky
whether winning or blown anxious days off course

there she suddenly is. And here he always is,
guiding her down with a tin of rattling corn,
not that she needs it, she knows him too, tethered
as she is by instinct or whatever you call it, family.
'Look at that,' he might just as well say, 'Look at that penguin.'

ALFIE IS A TRAIN IN THE DUCK-DUCK PARK

an express, a word he learnt from me,
the slowest member of the family, so
far away, headlong, by the pond if he
fell or someone took him how would
I get there, but this other train his younger
brother is on time behind me alongside
the playpark in this park which they run
to cross like this stopping only at London
and Sheffield Halloween University
not that Alfie looks like stopping

LARISSA AND SIENNA

In the cavernous old-fashioned back
of a Skoda Superb with its poor visibility,
the girls as they always will be. Lala, calm
behind (inside) a Peppa Pig stickerbook,
a year from being able to read, and Sisi
the big sister looking on, sideways,
just about to comment. The cavern
of a car holds them in their baby seats.
I could cry looking at them. The photo
is my screensaver and looking is
the wrong end of a telescope. I never knew
my grandparents and so I never knew.

WHAT WE DID ON OUR HOLIDAY

In the dark out of the rain with the donkeys
under the pier, Bluebell, Rose and snorting Daisy,
it's a day out from the days, beside the seaside
beside the sea that's actually an estuary
busy with trawlers, containers and the ferry
out of Hull. Then, when the August storm
won't blow over, we gather all our plastic colour
and run to the bright lights and looped blasts
of pop from the penny falls and two pence roulette
visual candy floss aural e-numbers just
what you want and indoor remote-control boats.
Next stop is the Leaking Boot for fish and chips.

Boarded up and always being done up, this is
Cleethorpes between the bird sanctuary and a big wheel
that was old even when the kids were young
and broke down with us rocking at the top.
The Promenade is snakes and ladders and hopscotch
far as ice cream and polystyrene tea as good as it gets.
It brightens sure enough on the land-train back
to the putting. I can still see our shadows
and the chance to explain rainbows in the
skirted round sprinklers. The last half hour
as is traditional is a toy from Beach Bargains
that will last as long as the day.

A GLOBE

in Y5, S Anselm's School, Bakewell

I am a globe
and *the* globe.

I light up sometimes.

I am mostly sea
and I'm all there is of land.

I'm a globe
in your classroom –

come here and spin
  night into day,
    calendrical.

Look at the places you know
and the so many more there are.

I hope you travel.

I hope you see me
  like now from outer space

a daytrip to the moon maybe
  or returning at slow light speed
    from a cruise in some far galaxy.

I'm a map made round
  to come back on itself.

I am a globe
  delighted that
    You are here.

KIOSK AT LADYBOWER

'Every Day Except Christmas Day'

She stands in a ten-foot galley
frying bacon. 7am in August
and still there seven at night. Sometimes
it's her mum, driving an hour in snow
to unlatch the shutter, light the gas.
The A-board stays out
among all those thousand acres
of deciduous and logging forest.
Easy to imagine a radio, a paperback.
If she leaves, if she ever leaves, imagine
doing this. Even first thing midweek, midwinter,
there's always someone glad to see the glow
and weekends it's thronged. (Drive Slowly –
Children and Ducks.) Footpaths go off
in all directions, up through history
and geology, keeping fit, walking
from friendship or grief or just instead.
And you and me, in among, a life
in our head like a printed page or unfolded
1:2500, with a torch if need be.

BOOKSHELVES

I

Books, enough for a dozen lifetimes,
a handful lived in till they fell apart
and two or three with parts of them
without meaning to got by heart. But most,
a thousand maybe, have stayed closed
or might as well, even dogeared whodunnits
I could take down again none the wiser.
Books read you they say or is it only poems.
Most of these are poems, slim volumes,
first editions worth pence or less and fat collecteds,
some that might yet come in for whichever
poor sod inherits the need of them. One
unputdownable sci-fi late at night the other day
made me jump, just as once I burst into tears
in the middle of *Zeno Was Here* in a café.

II *Stanley Cook*

And in the Longman Tennyson a bookmark
of essay titles in my tutor's typewriting,
which brings him back, brilliant, kind,
and wasted on us, those Harry Potter glasses
decades before the fact. He was a poet too,
though you wouldn't know: few read him then
and fewer still now. Their loss. Ours.
I crack the spine surprised again how alive
Alfred LT is in his pre-raph mausoleum
or necropolis in fact, where I wander
skin crawling as if for the first time.
He isn't here, they neither of them are,

but far away the noise of town begins again
and through rain on the bald street breaks the day.

III *Bookshelves Wallpaper in a Shed*

An outdoor indoors with four big squares
of hardbacks unrolled from a tube and pinned up
like a jigsaw, muzak. And which I love
because my daughter bought them. My daughter
and my other daughter whom I admire
more than all the books in Christendom,
and the two sons too if I can say that,
which I can here, in this library of lives
leather-bound and imaginary, blank
for the title and where the author would be.

IV

One must be a children's book to take them
walking in file out that door, suddenly
colourful, book after book after book down
the garden left turn at the gate and up
the street to its eponymous church,
with its sometime answers, or on into town
or a bus out from this bit of the universe
to the others, known and otherwise, waving
from its windows, opening its blocks of text
and saying *It's possible. Yes, you're here too.*

There for so long I never see them, laces
trailing over Dickens and George Eliot.
Also *The Day of the Jackal* – I remember
staying up on this same horsehair sofa
in a student house to finish it. And so
I go over. Dust on the ladder. I love
climbing among books and browsing
like a picture or giraffe in mid-air.
He wrote it in five weeks to make money
and straightaway (after four rejections)
was a millionaire. Frederick Forsyth.
He wrote it I see when I was in primary,
I remember the sloping pitch, can feel the itch
of the yellow cotton jersey. I lift
a boot while I'm up here. Thick dust
and baked-on mud, Nike unlike my
first pair which really were boots
with the studs nailed in, all of us chasing
the ball like a breeze. I never saw that
absence of strategy but bet Pete Betts did
and his dad, centre-forward for Sutton Town.
I saw them after school, father and son
booting a ball one touchline to the other.
There they are. And here I am with them
up a ladder with a book and a boot.

DARTER

Opportunity on the oche, that wonderful
Viking word oche, when there were still
working men in their clubs and the Legion
to watch the quarter final of the qualifiers,

when anyone and everyone could play the board
not the man and let the darts do the talking.
In the league you got a round in, part of your team,
then stood in the light when it was your time.

Hour after hour with the same three darts
thrown the same Zen way, week-in week-out
for the idea of a nine-dart checkout.
It could be done, but not by me, and so,

forty years ago, that quarter final, his calm
twelve darter was more than enough.
And so, like everyone, I turned to shake his hand,
and knew to turn my hand to something new.

Kenneth Koch for God's sake, Kenneth Koch
reading to twenty people in a room above a pub.
And not even poems, short plays. Crazy. Next day
he wheeled a suitcase into Huddersfield
buffet, three tennis racquets strapped to it
across the Atlantic, to meet for breakfast
on his way to York York. He was a person
not a book or memorial. He ate
a sandwich called a butty and drank tea
not coffee when in Rome, which he knew,
incidentally, like the back of his head.
It was before cameraphones. Behind that wall
with its artificial art a train
sweated and shivered. Behind that a second train
said something or other about fame,
which can only get up from the page
when the reader is content with
or without it. Of course he was a man,
but he spoke like a thoughtless boy. They all did,
and that was their greatness, not least the
reflection of a convex age, the great
that's to say among the great, and still
at the platform; another saw a river
of fish in the stream, much favoured, and the last
was the first to live only afterwards – on a beach –
who brought a brimming anecdote to his lips.
Remember? The day passed. A train
is just a vehicle. And suddenly it's evening.

D.H. LAWRENCE

You stayed put to us who lived practically next door,
a family anecdote, in Hucknall and Annesley.
But your gift your curse drove you in the end
as far as the Earth could go, kangaroo and snake,
Lady Asquith and Bertie Russell all alike to you.
Fine boned, free with your fists and Frieda
giving as good as she got, and Ottoline Morrell
who would not come till after you did
whatever you did. Chalk face not coal and even that
not for long because those who can do do
and you had your own airless dark to work in
like everyone just there, just then, in that choking
black with the whole of Sherwood Forest overhead.
Incandescent, inconsolable, a mardarse, you
were cut down by your temper, by so many
who couldn't see what you couldn't help but see.
Jessie Boot and Brian Clough, I thought but you
were more, out there with the literati: 'D H Lawrence:
Ezra Pound, you'll hate each other.' You wrote
fast against the spores that took your breath,
your lungs I mean, and didn't revise just ran
at it again. Quite properly shocked
by Casanova, you spoke for Lady Chatterley.
You'd no need for shame, though you were stung
by those rows of terraces, donkey-stone homes,
an evening river and giggling haystack next
to a slag-heap, still in their pit-dirt, still in their songs
your hands blue with ink their roaring songs
at the Badger Box, and my teenage aunt behind the bar
who thought you were noat, and who
though wrong was right to throw you out.

EMILY BRONTE

She bakes with a German grammar
propped open. Beyond the window an estate
of washing flaps in moorland. Beyond another
a graveyard whose trees speak rook, the hollow
darkness of her father's church. Cobbles walk down
to the steam railway, calling in with her
painted-out brother at one pub or another.
Ambition. Sup up. The tea rooms look out
from stoneware and fridge magnets. Her books
and her sisters are everywhere, too late
inoculate, her lyric with its lone green lane.
Her truest poem was fiction. The tapping
at the window's a village juke box
with six plays for 50p, the same wild
and windy 1970s. She admits her illness
in terror only hours before the last hour
on that roped-off midnight blue velveteen sofa.
Only our hearts and her heart coincide

THE HURST

for Ian Marchant and the Arvon Foundation

Here we are, laughing again, on the patio
in January of a mansion belonging
to an angry young man, Lord of the Manor
some time ago. Ian hands me the Oscar
while he rolls a cigarette, enjoying the stars.
Astrology he says is a way of mapping people.
He's a typical Libran. I'm a typical librarian.
Behind us a round table and walls of books
owned by a magician vanished and ongoing.
I know why people loved that man and have
some of his words by heart. I love the walks here
especially in snow especially through the woods,
I love the walks on paper we take in a group,
utterly and only ourselves, I love that line
of Les Murray's about the last line waiting
in the first. Also, I love walking in poems
betweentimes, opening a book like a window
at random and climbing into a room and time.
And just being here, which Ian knows better
than most, having been host. I don't need
to tell him, but I do. We're the same age,
me and Ian, twenty years younger than we are,
and not drunk, and slimmer, fitter, and altogether
better than ever, that being the way of words.

IN WINTER THE STEEP LANE

is often icy
one in four, and today
it brings me
to my hands and
dodgy knees

absurd under trees
tall as the sky
a mile or two to go

I crawl for a while
then scrabble
to my feet but stay low,

young old man
I stop at a dry
stone wall then step

up
atop
a stile

owl call
far city
constellation

then down
to a field
that might be snow

nothing to do
but keep going

MOON LIFE

A dome is the most
popular structure in the continual sun
of a sea named for an explorer:
there he is just by thinking.
Then you suit-up and lollop outdoors, Mr Bibendum.
How you got here who knows. Three weightless days
to this stepping-off point. Fibrebright
solar system and the first light years
beyond. And though there are others,
you don't meet almost never see, startling
when you do. Look at the stories
in the stars and the blue
planet scaled small to touch
that anybody rich enough might walk on.
At its worst now it's terror.
Breathless. Literally. Terror. And alone.
The boy in the bubble was an old song.
And then a mask, a distance.
Rocks are drilled into,
particles twist and turn,
precious ore, and in-drawn health;
we are people, not figures
in a word machine or numbers
on a graph in all this sea of space.

FLYING

after Leslie Norris

Falling is flying now and there's the river
of road, long as a piece of string, the A road North,
with on the right what you know of the sea,
and to the left sure enough mountains,
three cities. The wind changes note when you
turn your head. You go lower. Flip on your back,
lying for a while in the shallows of a holiday,
stratosphere, mesosphere, and beyond
the rest that just can't stop. You take a breath
and go lower, level out at an open book:
shopping centre, football field, swimming pool.
There's the school bus and as night follows day
the lane to the school, Long Lane, and for now
a bell tower with its bright chime. Pupils
or students throng at the gates like ghosts. One
looks up and sees you, and smiles, as if you might
look in at the window at Geography or listen
in the space between understanding to French
in the freeze and fry room, as if you might touch down
in the playground/carpark and find your feet,
joining in again for a little while, for now.

LANYARD

I

The wardrobe mirror in their room swings you out
beyond the precinct and the swimming pool
with all its voices in the roof. The fire station's
across the road and the ambulance service
like a soap though you never hear a siren.
You stand on the balcony of the maisonette.
Look down that road you used to know,
and there you are with your mum, wheeling her tartan bag
from bingo or sitting in the indoor market
at a table with glass coffee cups, never closer.
That winter your friend is seventeen like you
but somehow has learned to drive. It's a Saab,
just about, a car, white like the inch-thick snow
and the windscreen wipers don't work. But it goes
all the way to the Rifleman Volunteer
on New Years' Eve, where a girl in Lincoln green
and tights in this weather whispers in your ear.
When you lie in the road, it's summer again,
a book, a tan, a dayglo tent and a dozen bands
of new to the world music. A joss stick, a lava
lamp you take the top off and climb in, it isn't
what you expected, looking out, happy.

You wear a jacket with chalk in the pocket.
Someone pulls a lanyard into a noose. It's as exciting
as they say and suits you, already your hair.
A shoulder bag briefcase with dry markers
and marking, you wake two stations past home.
In a raked theatre they write down dates, lines
you flourish to remind them, how did someone

so long ago make all this with only 26 letters
and no screen not even a petrol engine
let alone Ryanair. You learn to abseil for charity
from the side of Z Block, ten storeys. You never
get the hang of the whiteboard but are first
to the photocopier. The textbook with the tiring house
of prodigious memory. You live in the canteen,
821, you and Nick Drake. The volumes are hardback
and open with a creak, sprout slips of paper in your hands
with facts and conjecture. You lie down in the pond
because it's also summer. What you see you never say.
The fear and joy expand but you're looking
the other way. The mirror is all you are and almost
everyone. At some stage this becomes a loft
extension and cellar conversion with a few hundred
square miles of country in between. You take
a wrong turn but it's still early. You don't know
and press on, and when you realise you press on.

Abruptly you're shrinking. Even you notice
though you see it every day, like sneaking up.
It's because you are old, older, oldest.
Somebody's sex life for so long in your head
takes up residence in another part of the body
though unfortunately not that one. At night
the sky is full of mostly black, then two or three
binary stars, so many more than you knew
and none of them visible to the naked eye.
So, July, you stand last thing with binoculars
and look at one phase of the moon in particular
where someone from the future or a picture book
waves and you wave back forgetting magnification
is only ever one way. You might just as well whisper.

At other times the sky comes down to the lake
beside a wood beyond a cornfield. It's a blue
sky or appears so and it presses against the water.
The water is plastic among other things. At one time,
it would be ice, even the river, so thick the town
skated on it and set up a fair with buckets of fire,
figure 18 in an Introduction to an age of drama.
You're at the far end of this it seems. The little shovel
is plastic too he clears the windscreen with
before the engine starts first time. The snow
becomes flakes like a simile and you manage
to get there only stopping once to clear the air.

II

That's a feather in your cap you tell her. I can't
believe you said that, she says for the third time.
You're the poor and she's the principal boy
you notice not Maid Marion. You run for a moment
through Sherwood with the harriers, Sunday morning
rain or shine, never more fit or quite fast enough.
The ambulance station doors are concertina blue
and open like a horse race. The pirate radio is out
at sea and comes and goes, like the land-
locked lighthouse you set out to with your friends
at throwing-out time, till just before morning
dreams break in as you walk back. Back
from the Derwent, oil-beautiful with rowing boats,
the splash and drift, splash and hollow drift
of slow-moving water, a level calm expressed as years;
the cliffside handhold's a hundred feet up and you
panic, stopped, unable, until one way, then another,

you talk yourself down ten yards, twenty, to a ledge,
a path your eyes adjust to, and you can breathe,
sweat drying on your back, back to a lane, lamplight
and brilliant ropes of coloured bulbs in the park,
where the night waits it out with ghosts and dust.

Lit by laburnum you sit at the end of the bed
of somebody's grave, at one far side of town
with a takeaway tea, in an impromptu
or by-product leisure space, not getting the hang
of me-time, Grenoside Woods behind you, like a job
you drove to for three decades or three days.
A latecomer runs in with flowers, colour to add
to the year-round colour. Somewhere your aunties
are sewing a white apron for science in big school
in September. You won't see them again until
it's grandchildren making that step up is it
to chemistry labs and life-long language labs,
a summer all-weather field beyond the furnace.
Who could remember you better? Your hopes
come back like a board game or marble run.
You spent most of those years with tables
of irregular verbs and if you never learned
to make yourself understood, nobody minded.
Laburnum is a tree, a small tree but even so
a light-source and the bed it seems to shade
might well be your own, or one just like it.
The lanyard meanwhile is a badge of office.
You put your head in like taking a medal
perhaps even the gold, ok, not the gold,
but you were there, fifteen minutes, long enough
it transpires to look up, coming round to a sea
of careful faces, listening to the music.

The sky bumps its head on your head. The night
remembers, and what it says is, There's only today,
and the ache means at least there's some left.
The clock every hour a different bird call, who knows
which it will be, who'd want to know, even the owl.